THE WISDOM OF A STARRY NIGHT

Using the Power of Great Art for Self-Awareness

THE WISDOM OF A STARRY NIGHT
* Using the Power of Great Art for Self-Awareness *

* SHARON MARSON *

BARNES & NOBLE

NEW YORK

For Jay
my North Star, who has been with me every step of the way guiding my vision

And for our children
the brightest points in our constellation

✳ ✳

2006 Barnes & Noble Books

ISBN 0-7607-7098-0

Printed and bound in China

06 07 08 09 M 9 8 7 6 5 4 3 2 1

"Twenty years from now you will
be more disappointed by
the things that you didn't do
than by the ones you did do.
So throw off the bowlines.
Sail away from the safe harbor.
Catch the trade winds in your sails.
Explore. Dream. Discover."

—*Mark Twain*

epiphany (epiphania), **n.** a usually sudden manifestation or perception of the essential nature or meaning of something; an intuitive grasp of reality through something usually simple and striking; an illuminating discovery; a revealing scene or moment

Looking at a Starry Night

How often have you had a moment of complete clarity where you've known your heart's desire, glimpsed your deepest self, recognized the best path, or just felt a sense of wholeness and well-being, only to have that moment of epiphany escape you in the busyness and details of life? Perhaps that knowing moment occurred on vacation while admiring a starry night, or during a quiet moment at home before anyone else was awake, or while reading something that touched your heart.

The Wisdom of a Starry Night is a vehicle to take you back to the insightful moments that contain a vision of your best and deepest self—to an understanding that provides guidance and acts as the impetus for transformation, a medium for metamorphosis. It is a return to your essential nature and to what holds true meaning for you. This unique approach uses visual imagery in tandem with meaningful inquiry to prompt an internal shift. Specifically, the experience of viewing soul-stirring masterpieces, along with being open to the accompanying thought-provoking musings, furnishes the scene or moment to awaken you and launch your imagination on a journey to a place inside where those times of epiphany can be revisited. Visual imagery and self-reflection provide a window to your inner world, allowing you to view what is often overlooked and giving you a self-portrait to work toward manifesting.

This book is an outgrowth of my years doing post-graduate work in education. As an educator I have been intrigued by what promotes creative processes in children, and how we can develop curriculum that uses creative thinking to move them to greater self-understanding and insight. Creative thinking need not be daunting. It is a skill, and like any other skill, it can be learned and practiced. It comprises four components: fluency, the ability to produce many ideas in various categories; flexibility, generating a wide range of ideas on one topic; originality, developing unique and unusual responses; and elaboration, adding ideas, providing details, and extending thinking. To help children gain facility in these four sub-skills I expose them to divergent thinking by repeatedly presenting them with open-ended questions—questions that have no right or specific answers. All replies are accepted, and as children become more comfortable taking risks and being momentarily suspended in the ambiguous, they become better at allowing a newfound vision to emerge and at gaining access to their personal awareness.

At the same time I implemented this methodology I made a practice of displaying art masterpieces. We worked toward understanding various artists' styles, exploring both the genius of their work and the trajectory they took as they expressed themselves throughout their lives. Discussions about the paintings evoked emotional responses. When I saw how individually effective these two systems were in promoting creative processes, and as I observed children's thinking becoming more fluent, flexible, original, and elaborate, it occurred to me that combining the two modalities might carry the children further than either could do on its own. I proceeded to couple stimulating questions with the viewing of artworks and found there was exponential growth in the children's abilities to engage in creative process and come to epiphany, as could be seen in the wisdom and the expressiveness of the children's answers.

As an example, see what happened when I asked the following question while showing van Gogh's *Starry Night*:

What wisdom can you imagine finding looking at a starry night?

there's magic in life
Michael, age 6

* * * * * * * * * * * * * * * * * * *

that everything dies
and everything's born
Madeline, age 5

* * * * * * * * * * * * * * * * * * *

to remember that they'll
always be shooting stars
Rina, age 5

The wisdom the children so eloquently expressed in response to inquiry and art was often breathtaking, creating in itself a moment of art through the beauty that was conveyed. The children, ages 5 and 6, were able to tap into their inner resources and release what was within. They had an intuitive grasp of reality that led them to an illuminating discovery.

When the door to creative thinking opens it transports all of us, not just children, to the way we thought long before we went to school. It is not all that dissimilar from what artists, scientists, and inventors do. In looking at how creative children are and how free their minds and imaginations can be, we gain insight into how humans are built. Though these pathways in our brain may have been suppressed to various degrees for a variety of reasons, including acculturation, they can be reawakened.

I asked people of varying ages the same question: "What wisdom can you imagine finding looking at a starry night?" Take a look at what people expressed when art and language were presented in unison. Their responses prove the power of this tool for all ages; regardless of one's years, a childlike enchantment can be recaptured.

"the wisdom within" —*Tamar, age 14*

"life is a cycle" —*Enid, age 70*

"there's wonder in the universe"—*David, age 47*

Just as I present children and adults with replicas of paintings while asking probing questions, so I do the same for you. You will find the question on the left-hand side of the page, the image on the right. Look at the painting while also exploring the inquiry. Take time to reflect, to ponder. Allow the visual experience to interface with what is triggered by the question. Both your left brain and your right brain will be engaged this way.

Everyone has two cerebral hemispheres, left and right, that make up one brain. They are connected by bundles of nerves that cross the midline and through which the two parts speak to each other. In looking at the qualities of the left brain and right brain, we can see how both hemispheres are in use when language and art, too often kept apart, are put together.

LEFT BRAIN	RIGHT BRAIN
verbal	visual
logical	creative, intuitive
attention to detail	looks at the whole
likes to ask questions	likes to answer questions
learns through discussions	learns through visual prompts
analyzes	synthesizes

This book creates opportunities for both halves of the brain to be activated and to communicate. It is an exercise in simultaneous stimulation of both hemispheres, training the brain to work in synchrony. As our eyes read the artwork as well as the words, more than one modality is employed and the two halves interact, engaging the whole person. *The Wisdom of a Starry Night* is an active process; it is an experience. We bring to it ourselves, our suppositions, and the framework through which we see the world. The imagery and questions provide interaction with our innermost selves, evoking and bringing forward what's hidden inside.

The Wisdom of a Starry Night is a bridge to the essential that lies within you. It is a vision quest that inspires realization, discovery, and wonder. In this book I blend the viewing of many masterpieces with inquiry in order to elicit creative process and facilitate movement toward epiphany. You will find it to be a springboard for opening conversations, making connections, and deepening relationships between friends, spouses, lovers, family members, and oneself. Sometimes answers will come to the fore immediately; sometimes you will want to contemplate the inquiry over time. The questions will probe the boundaries of who you are, and you may be surprised by some of your replies. Sample responses, from people of all ages, are located in the back of the book. The delightful openness of others can facilitate your journey.

As van Gogh said, "For my part I know nothing with any certainty, but the sight of the stars makes me dream." And so I ask again: "What wisdom can you imagine finding looking at a starry night?"

What do you see when you look inside yourself?

When do you feel like time flies?

Who would you most like to sit with here?
Why?

Where do you feel rooted?

**What would you like
to take a first step toward?**

With whom do you share your secrets?

**When in life do you
feel you hit the bull's-eye?**

What runs through your veins?

What is your version of freedom?

When do you feel most whole?

HMATISSE 52

When is your heart open?

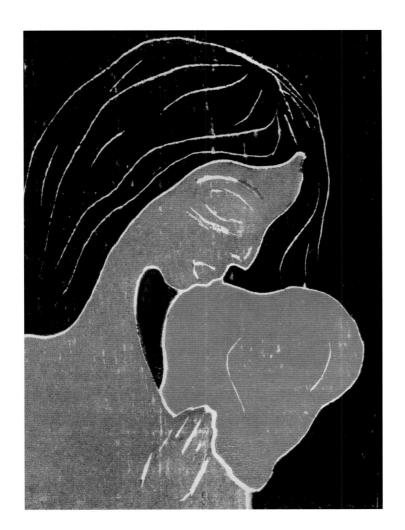

How do you express love?

It's said it takes a village to raise a child. Who are you glad to have had in your village?

With whom would you like to reconnect?

When do you feel liberated?

When do you feel at peace?

When do you feel you are carrying the weight of the world?

When have you been
pulled in different directions?
What did you choose? Why?

Who can you count on to go to bat for you?
Who would you go to bat for?

In what ways do you show kindness?

With all that you juggle each day
how do you keep balanced?

Who is in your inner circle?

**When do you feel you're
on the outside looking in?**

What dreams do you have for yourself?

What wisdom can you imagine
finding looking at a starry night?

The lion arrived without leaving footprints.
When have you experienced the miraculous?

In what do you lose yourself?

What is your sanctuary?

For what are you grateful?

Who do you feel watches over you?

When you get very quiet what calls to you?

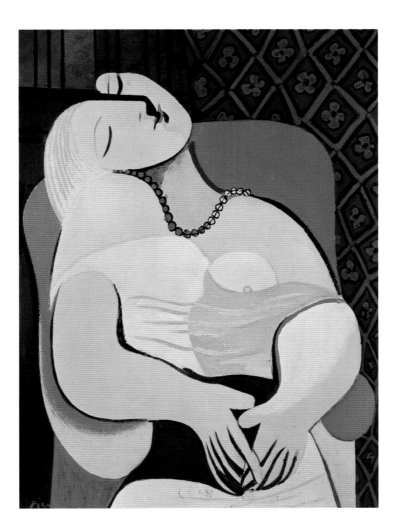

What is your vision of
yourself one year from now?
How about five years from now?

What do you wish to become?

If you could walk through any door
what would you like it to open to?

What do you feel is the most important question you can ask yourself?

What imprint do you want to leave in the world?

SAMPLE RESPONSES

✴ *What do you see when you look inside yourself?*

A big heart. —*Sharona, age 5*

Pablo Picasso: *Girl Before a Mirror (Femme au miroir)*, 1932

✴ *Who would you most like to sit with here? Why?*

My Uncle Georgie who died. —*Drew, age 6*

Jamie Wyeth: *Island Library*

✴ *When in life do you feel you hit the bull's-eye?*

When I say the right thing to the right person at the right time. —*Eric, age 29*

Jasper Johns: *Target on an Orange Field*, c. 1957

★ *When do you feel liberated?*

On the last day of school. —*Aaron, age 13*

Henri Matisse: *Icarus, Plate VII from "Jazz,"* 1947

★ *When do you feel at peace?*

When I know my intentions have been good. —*Harriet, age 71*

Henri Matisse: *Reclining Nude in a White Dress*, 1946

★ *Who is in your inner circle?*

My family, my Mom, my sister through birth, my sister through marriage, and my sisters and brothers through life. —*Sharon, age 44*

Paul Gauguin: *Conversation (Les Parau Parau)*, 1891

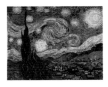

* *What wisdom can you imagine finding looking at a starry night?*

The wisdom that everything works out just the way it's supposed to, that every moment is an opportunity to do good, and that the world is full of possibility. —*Martha, age 45*

Vincent van Gogh: *The Starry Night*, 1889

* *In what do you lose yourself?*

Memories. —*Rosalie, age 81*

Gustav Klimt: *Fulfilment (Die Erfullung)*, detail of Stoclet Frieze, c.1905-1909

* *For what are you grateful?*

For many, many things, including my life being enriched and my understanding deepened by meeting people who inspire me by living in ways I aspire toward. —*Benyamin, age 36*

Henry Ossawa Tanner: *The Thankful Poor*, 1894

✳ *When you get very quiet what calls to you?*

My life's purpose. —*Sheryl, age 39*

Pablo Picasso: *The Dream (La reve)*, 1932

✳ *What is your vision of yourself one year from now? How about five years from now?*

One year: having greater awareness of what's eternal, boundless, perfect; in five, benefiting others by sharing it. —*Talya, age 50*

Alberto Giacometti: *Self Portrait*, 1921

✳ *What do you wish to become?*

A kinder person. —*Avital, age 33*

Caspar David Friedrich: *Woman at Dawn*

If you could walk through any door what would you like it to open to?

A world of peace, where people's hearts are open to love and their eyes to truth. —*Murray, age 74*

Edward Hopper: *Rooms by the Sea*, 1951

What do you feel is the most important question you can ask yourself?

How can I best, in this moment, bring heaven closer to earth? —*Abe, age 69*

Edvard Munch: *Young Woman on the Beach. The Lonely One*, 1896

What imprint do you want to leave in the world?

Love. —*Gila, age 5*

M.C. Escher: *Puddle*, 1952

CREDITS

(Arranged in order of appearance in the book.)

Pablo Picasso (1881-1973) © 2005 Estate of Pablo Picasso/ Artists Rights Society, NY. *Girl Before a Mirror (Femme au miroir),* 1932. Oil on canvas, 64 x 51 ¼ in. Gift of Mrs. Simon Guggenheim. (2.1938) The Museum of Modern Art, New York, NY, U.S.A. Digital Image © The Museum of Modern Art/Licensed by SCALA/ Art Resource, NY

Marc Chagall (1887-1985) © Artists Rights Society, NY/ ADAGP, Paris. *Time is a River Without Banks (Le Temps n'a point de rives),* 1930-1939. Oil on canvas, 39 ⅜ x 32 in. Given anonymously. (612.1943) The Museum of Modern Art, New York, NY, U.S.A. Digital Image © The Museum of Modern Art/Licensed by SCALA/Art Resource, NY

Jamie Wyeth (1946-) *Island Library.* Art © Jamie Wyeth. Watercolor on paper, 22 x 30 in.

Frida Kahlo (1907-1954) © 2005 Banco de México Diego Rivera & Frida Kahlo Museums Trust. Av. Cinco de Mayo No.2, Col. Centro, Del. Cuauhtémoc 06059, México, D.F. *Portrait of Luther Burbank (Retrato de Luther Burbank),* detail, 1931. Photograph © The Art Archive/Dolores Olmedo Mexico/Dagli Orti

Vincent van Gogh (1853-1890) *First Steps, after Millet,* 1890. Oil on canvas, 28 ½ x 35 ⅞ in. The Metropolitan Museum of Art, Gift of George N. and Helen M. Richard, 1964. (64.165.2) Photograph © 1999 The Metropolitan Museum of Art

Winslow Homer (1836-1910) *Two Boys Rowing,* 1880. Watercolor. Private Collection. Photograph © Art Resource, NY

Jasper Johns (1930-) *Target on an Orange Field,* c. 1957. Art © Jasper Johns: Licensed by VAGA, New York, NY, U.S.A. Watercolor, pencil on paper. 11 x 8.5 in. The Museum of Contemporary Art, Los Angeles. Bequest of Marcia Simon Weisman.

Giorgio de Chirico (1888-1978) © Artists Rights Society, NY/SIAE, Rome. *The Scholar's Playthings,* 1917. Oil on canvas, 35 ¼ x 20 ¼ in. The Minneapolis Institute of Arts, Gift of Mr. and Mrs. Samuel H. Maslon. (72.75) Photograph © The Minneapolis Institute of Arts

Keith Haring (1958-1990) © The Estate of Keith Haring. *Untitled (for the American Ballet),* 1988

Henri Matisse (1869-1954) © 2005 Succession H. Matisse, Paris/Artists Rights Society, NY. *Blue Nude III,* 1952. Private collection. Photo © Giraudon/Art Resource, NY

Edvard Munch (1863-1944) © 2005 The Munch Museum/ The Munch-Ellingsen Group/Artists Rights Society, NY. *The Girl and the Heart,* 1898-99 Woodcut. Munch Museum, Oslo, Norway. Photo © Munch Museum (Andersen/de Jong)

Gustav Klimt (1862-1918) *The Three Ages of Woman (Die drei Lebensalter der Frau),* detail, 1905. Oil on canvas. Galleria

ACKNOWLEDGMENTS

With deep gratitude to: my husband and children, my Mom, sister, in-laws, and nieces for believing in me and patiently listening to my questions; my grandfather, Abe Silverman (z"l), for providing answers; my friends who support me, share the journey, and live in my heart: Barbara Feld, Sheryl Haut, Gloria Iodice, Leslie Maron, and Sy Kolitch (z"l), who undoubtedly advocates for me from on high, Rena Rossman, Yosefa Sarlin, the Schaums, Stuart and Wendy Simons, Robin Yucht, Alan and Janet Rosenthal, angels, who teach me it's possible to grow wings; Rav Elazar Kenig, Reb Efraim Kenig, and Talya Lipshutz of Tsfat with whom I'm blessed to connect; my mentors at S.A.R. Academy: Marcia Jacobowitz, Harriet Levin, and Rabbi Yamin Goldsmith who generously share their time, encouragement, and keen insight; and my students, who inspire me by being vanguards in questioning and thinking without constraint.

I direct any good that comes from this work back to the One, the Only One, who puts the stars in the sky and is the Source of all wisdom.